The Next Breath

poems by

Richard Sime

Finishing Line Press
Georgetown, Kentucky

The Next Breath

Copyright © 2023 by Richard Sime
ISBN 979-8-88838-232-5 First Edition
All rights reserved under International and Pan-American Copyright Conventions.
No part of this book may be reproduced in any manner whatsoever without written permission from the publisher, except in the case of brief quotations embodied in critical articles and reviews.

Publisher: Leah Huete de Maines
Editor: Christen Kincaid
Cover Art: Boyce Benge
Author Photo: Charles Mohacey
Cover Design: Elizabeth Maines McCleavy

Order online: www.finishinglinepress.com
also available on amazon.com

Author inquiries and mail orders:
Finishing Line Press
P. O. Box 1626
Georgetown, Kentucky 40324
U. S. A.

Table of Contents

Twenty Twenty xi

PART ONE

Visitors 1
Dinner, for Two 2
The principal 3
The Usual 4
Away 6
Fatherhead 7
What Comes Next 8

PART TWO

The Drawing 13
Dogged 14
At Pepe's 15
Touch 16
Self-Portrait in a Burnt Pizza 17
Museum of Natural History 18
The Retreat 19

PART THREE

Blue Venom Balls 23
The Happy Hour 26
For All Time 27
Before Stonewall After 28
Wilderness 30
An Iceless Arctic 31
Provincetown Song 32
Hands 33

PART FOUR

Grit 37
Grown Men 38
draped on the bed 39
Moules Frites 40
Doesn't 41
Pathways 42
Marilyn in Minnesota 43
So Tender an Hour 44
Text to Text 45
Love 47

PART FIVE

Fine Arts Work Center 51
Another Summer 52
Into the Valley 53
Gathered 55
My Mother's Breasts 56
On We Went 57
Brother Eyes 59
for good 60
Paco, Brother, and Me 61
The Keepers 63
Gleason's Beach 64

Missive 66

ACKNOWLEDGMENTS 67

BIOGRAPHY 68

*For Boyce Benge, painter, writer, mentor,
who freely gave me love and spiritual support
when I most needed it, truly helping to save my life.*

ABOUT THE COVER

Detail from Missive, Boyce Benge, 2007. Acrylic on paper.

Photo courtesy Charles Mohacey

An abstract expressionist who came to New York City from North Carolina in the 1950s, Boyce Benge (1929-2016) evolved into a painter of text-based works using a wide range of writings—political, religious, poetic, twelve-step, memoir. The detail of the painting from which the cover of this book is taken is based on the poem "Missive," which brings *The Next Breath* to its end.

Twenty Twenty

Whom the gods love dies young —Herodotus

They say the polar vortex has broken,
May, just 33 degrees this morning
with sunshine all day long until a sudden
flurry of old grey snowflakes turning

into a rain slid down my window glass.
But now the sun blasts out again,
hot and yearning, like me here in these rays
of summer as I gaze across the Hudson

and the sun draws back into that grey, which
suits this year of plague harvesting the old,
infirm, hale youth, children too, blood, flesh
like my own. It struck me as well, here, alone,

yet I, at seventy-five, why've I survived?

PART ONE

Visitors

There are two of them, though he suspects
they may be one, two sides of some same coin.
Scent
      showed up first, in the corner
of what became his tv room, triangular,
intimate, a closet when he moved in
but with the largest window in the house,
six huge panes of glass. A yellow smell, sweet,
dry, plastic. Out went the old vinyl shade
but the odor crawled back through the doorless
doorway to his bedroom, then downstairs
to the living room where he lay that day
the other showed up:
                Draft, off his left
on his shoulder hip leg, niggling and wet.
He blocked the fireplace up, lay
under piles of cushions, blankets, but it took
hot showers to rid the chill, not for long when
that winter the inside plexiglass storms
blew down, snow through the seams of bare glass.
He replaced every window in every room,
double-paned glass, yet wisps
of the two remain,
           a lick of welcome
that has spread to all the rooms, to the walk
outside, even into his car, sickly
insinuating itself everywhere
until his taste and even touch are tetched.
Sometimes he can sense their approach, restless
twins who reach into the corners of
waiting rooms at his ear-nose-throat doc,
even his shrink, moldering out there where
they're dying…or where they've just been born.

Dinner, for Two

The plains surround us, treeless
and flat as the countertop
I'm sitting at. Wind, a lot of it,
shakes the winter day as my mother breaks
the eggs into a soup bowl, sprinkles in I don't know what,
hand-beats it thick, old silver fork on
old china, pours in some milk.

The skillet is heating on the stove,
she drops in a chunk of butter
and with her fork guides it
side-to-side around the steaming pan.

The bread is plain white, store-bought,
wrapped in waxed paper printed red and white
in a pattern like the cloth on a cafe table.
She dips each slice in the batter, lets the yellow drain,
toasts it just right without burning, a scatter
of brown islands in a sea of gold,
slides it with her spatula to my plate.

Dad won't let her buy real maple syrup
so we use the stuff from a little
log cabin made of tin, a sticky lid on the roof
where the chimney ought to be.

She doesn't make any for herself, but
have as much as you want, she tells me. More,
I say, and she pulls out
two slices, puts one in the batter.
More batter too. She shakes her head but leaves
the bread soak longer. I like the way she likes
to watch me eat her French toast, though

she's never been to France. I can see us in a funny
French car, top down, thin tall trees behind us. She makes
more batter. Six slices. Eight. Her eyes grow big. What
would Dad say? But we know what he doesn't know
won't hurt.

The principal

bursts into the classroom & though there may be nothing
but the sound of door banging open,
the child hears a squeal of wheels, steam
hissing, whoop of siren
as that man barrels in, a blur of thrust & steel, but this
is just sixth grade & the target of his wrath
some brat of twelve who heaved his fist
into the gut of Miss Keller & the child in his desk
at the back of the room tries not to see that man
who lifts his hand & strikes the boy again
as the man with whom he'll sit tonight for dinner,
the man who once would pull him down
chocolate mints from a box on the top shelf in his closet,
the man who too swung his hand at him
that one time the child remembers, as he sits still
at his desk, sinking hard into the wood

The Usual

The drive begins on gravel, Dakota gravel,
ends on gravel too, the boy seated in back, his dad
driving as usual, his mom talking, quiet
("She's your mother," he can hear her say).

They get to blacktop, his dad stops in a town
they always drive straight through, leaves, returns,
drops a brown paper bag on the floor.
"Okay?" he says, and drives.
No more talk—how long these mute trips last!—
until they reach the graveled turn to Northwood and,
beyond the cold brown fields, her house.

It's on the corner, a half-step up to the porch
she'll be waiting on just as they arrive,
her home creaking and groaning inside the old wood
his dad and a brother built it with years ago,
recycled, like she is now, off the farm into town.

Behind the house, a sagging barn, inside it
two adjoining dry toilets of wood, a lid on each hole,
which, with her kitchen sink, amounts to her bathroom.
In the parlor next to her doorless bedroom
sits a silver clock, ticking, ticking, loud and grey.

She always makes the meal but today
his dad hands her the brown bag, sits down alone
in the parlor and reads *The Gleaner*.
Usually they sit there and talk Norwegian but she's gone,
his mom comes in with more bags, heads
right into the kitchen. No one is left but the boy.

He goes outside, sits on the lid of her cistern
where she chills her food put inside a cage she lowers
on a rope into the ground. He sits and sits, time
stretching out far around him,
goes back inside through the kitchen door.

No one, just the door to the stairway upstairs where
if they stay the night, he and his brother sleep.
He opens it. On the steep rise, she sits
(Julia is her name, no one ever uses it), apron open,
the bag flattened on her lap, cans of beer
lying askew, save for the one pressed
to her lips. *"Namen!"* she yells in her Norwegian,
flopping across the beers to shield them.

He runs, doesn't know where, doesn't recall the meal
or sitting alone in the back on the drive home,
as if all the usual had ended,
she at the kitchen sink pumping cold water
into a pot to heat for the dishes,
the dizzy tilt of floors and doors, must-
scented doilies pinned to every arm and headrest,
her bed peering at the parlor
through the doorway curtain, the grey
grey light, the clock's
tick, tick, tick.

Away

There the lake lay, fat yet twisted into a cleft
in the Olympic foothills, Sitka spruce
a loden cascade down the slopes to water
blue from afar, green up close the days
we rowed to the farthest shores. Yes,
at last we were here; we could do this.

At night in the lodge we played
double solitaire, a furious slamming
of red cards on black in the firelight,
everyone, the whole world, watched. Yes,
whenever we wanted, we could do this.

Our mothers wore bright jackets, hair
splayed grey and white in the photos we took,
no color film. But color surrounded us,
buttery sun some days, and in low clouds
and rain a gentle lavender. Yes,
we could swim in the rain, too.

No driving, though the sharp white
peaks beckoned—they looked
so young and tall down upon us—
but this was a time of idle pleasures.
Water, wind, laughter. No fathers.

Fatherhead

Eyes steel ice, jaw set, lips pulled thin,
forehead flushed, brows knit, temples

throbbing, palms sweating, cheeks
ballooned—Dixieland, the slide

trombone his escape—neck cologned,
fingers curled, that ring his signet.

~~~

His fist now limp, hair a wave of
black gone white overnight, chest

de-brawned, arms pasty, hips sheeted,
ankles bare and chafed, his lungs a

clacking bellows by his side, oh
father, alone in this room, wife

absent, children fled, this bed your
bier, heart a bone, broken.

What Comes Next

How far can he get? Paris, he once thought,
the land of the Franks coming into view as the sun lifted
from the ocean, Europa, of which he knew so much so little
but New York is easier, a city scattered on islands
though seldom is he aware of the sea
the grand liners are gone no foghorns at night
everyone arrives by bus or train or plane
he can do whatever he wants
no minders.

~~~

It was the rain,
an entire winter of rain,
then the betrayal,
her life's dream, the mountains
of green trees, the sea beyond them
gone now to desert,
his choice, the husband-man's choice,
stunt-treed Arizona, the dry
remains of an ancient sea.

Her son so far away, born amid the islands
and peninsulas of Puget Sound—
she had told him of her first times there,
the thrill of feeling her way in the fog
across the Manette Bridge, mist on her face,
her skin would drink it up with a smile
at the coast, beachcombing treasures
she would mount into a seascape
or make into a serpent
rearing its serpent head
of glued stone eyes
from driftwood.

The trips from the prairie to the sea
had never been yearly, each second or third year
the vestigial family would make
the half-continent drive the husband-father

drove, he picked the route, the hour
of departure and arrival,
brief stays in a pretty place
begrudged, she had no choice but
get back in the car and leave.

In the desert they live in HUD housing,
low-slung townhomes, barracks-like
patios walled in by cinder blocks,
a bedroom for each, one bath,
bloody urine is the start,
his wish to die, her
assigned role to let it happen,
where is she, her son
wonders, there
in her room crying.

"Thank you, Jesus," she says
when the hospital calls,
she will wear happy colors,
no viewing, no ashes,
they were not allowed
by the state of Arizona, she,
left alone, beached
in the desert,
untrained to take his place.

~~~

It takes a year until she asks,
when will I ever see the ocean again?
Could the son make it happen, he makes trips
to San Francisco for his own pleasure,
but there's a coastline, up in Sonoma he's been told,
a few hours' drive, the Pacific
chewing off pieces of land abandoned
to the breakers, sheer cliffs down
to white water, fog every morning
and a mile or two into the hills
pure sun, the aroma of eucalyptus,
the vineyards, the wines,

the drinking, the mother's morning
climb down seventy-eight stairs to the water,
the son's hangovers at surf's edge,
the successful sister comes, the beaten-down
black-sheep brother, the dutiful son
on his slow descent just as AIDS is arising,
a dam has been breached,
some new kind of family emerging
but into what?

PART TWO

The Drawing

I'm not an artist but I make a drawing anyway
After all, it was our first encounter
She was raised in that kennel
An old trailer on a hill
But what I draw looks tilted on its rear end
There's plenty light but little shade
I add some frenchified shadow around the trailer
A loud squeak, ka-pow! its door is opened
I watch, standing in the foreground
But I can't draw me either
A stick figure descends the trailer's steps
Dark, writhing mass on its hip
What have I gotten into?
The figure approaches me
The mass takes shape
Head   Tail   Paws
She's thrust into my arms
I can't draw passion, shoved aside
One day I'll weep into her belly
Perspective is a gift I haven't mastered

Dogged

I step inside his room, so far from the town
he comes from. Small town, like my own I expect,
but in Iowa. These roaches, I expect them too.
They've lived with him since he followed me here.
He can't shake them.
                      I can't shake him: Lone
window on far wall, crown molding askew,
dark mounds floating in the gloom. I shine
my light—a heap of clothes feet deep, piles
of shopping bags, a broken lamp, dishes.
On a bit of bare floor, a thin stiff rug and skanky
pillow. "Lotusland," I think. I step no further
but can't stop staring—
                          evicted from Chelsea
to Jamaica (the Queens one), was there
a time I loved him? Loved…so long ago.

At Pepe's

I have pepperoni. You, vegetable.
No cheese, you're working at being vegan,
I'm trying to be low carb, neither one
doing too well at it. We're friends, good friends
of a certain kind of space. A big one,
geographic. Smaller one, age. Still kids
in our own ways. Wary of the other,
or is that just me?
                        When you start to cry
I'm not surprised, though till now you've never
let me see one tear. Yesterday you said
laughter's just like crying. My insults make
you laugh, me too. They keep the distance fresh
yet close, but not too near.
                              Am I too old
for love, or just sex? Never found the bridge
from one to the other. There is one, no?
That is why you're crying. Your bridge is gone,
this is a chance to be brand-new, I tell you,
shed old selves you're used to.
                                   I'd like to be
new too. Too lazy, too worn out, but here
I am with you, crying. I wonder at
the way we cry, your tears on overflow,
mine inside a smile. Tomorrow you'll leave
lighter, brighter. Me, happy to be free.

Touch

June, the evening light in Paris lingers long
as we enter the opera at Bastille to see
Le crépuscule des dieux. Nearby, a hawker
of programs, Proust-like, his suit too tight, his
sticky, liquid voice pulling me to linger as
it drives me insane. I need your care,
you step near, lead me away. How well you
know me though we seldom touch, at times a hug
from some remove. Yet your hand on my arm feels
intime, as outside the windows, daylight turns
deep red, like the Sangre de Cristo above Santa Fe
after a rain. We've been to Glyndebourne,
the Garnier, and here one more *Götterdammerung*
within the thirty years we've been friends, half
your life, less of mine. How I crave this touch.

Self-Portrait in a Burnt Pizza

The parmigiana has vaporized, the flat disk spread
Char-black as that vision you had last night
Seeking your reflection & seeing nothing
But the old earth burnt flat as you drew it forth
From that heat, no, this heat, the heat I feel now
In which I actually see myself, or is it you,
Rising on the hot waves to my hungry face, our face,
The two of us one, and then there's her, she of the four paws
Toe-nailing the floor, she too eating out there
In her white ovular bed, does this make us a trio, the crunch
Of her teeth echoing off the parlor walls though
I can't rise to look, don't need to rise, don't want to rise,
Locked here at the table with this fractured disk
Gazing up at me, my hunger overwhelming the vile
Transubstantiated cheese, the tomato breath beneath turned
Sludge, like exhausted oil clogging pistons, cylinders
As I, you, she rip my/our/her teeth through to...
Crust! we can all recognize that, can't we, but can we
Savor it, can we two, too, chomp with the brio of the four-
Legged one, the image of our selves flecking from our lips
Black as the pepper you overspread your soup today,
You always do, I tell you beware but ahead you go, impulsive
As dog out there, she'll eat anything, well maybe not
Anchovies, the last I found on the kitchen floor,
Much better when she grazes weeds in the spring, the
Floss of her vomit across the greening blades
Swaying along the pathway as she veers off into woods
Where I dread what she'll mouth before returning
To lick my hand, we're all animals, you & I
Even more than she, we have history, we have self-awareness,
We are civilized, this smoldering black mirror pledging us &
All them out there too, just to this for which it stands

Museum of Natural History

She's one of the odor-seeking scamps of the evening,
her nasal passages swollen, neural circuits
pulsing, tail raised as she tugs a 70ish
gent, a malted milkshake in his hand, along the wide walk
that surrounds the rock- and iron-walled square.

Dog/human/rat rot trellises the air.

She has a name, but he calls her
sweetheart, darling, honey, this terrier
scrambling under the slats of a bench surrounded
by uncanned garbage where
the odd yank of leash keeps her from grazing.

They'll walk the entire perimeter, fourteen city blocks,
traffic flowing by in nighttime languor,
she intent upon the scents, he thinking, thinking, thinking.

Here, he once lived right here on this street that dead-ends
at the caboose of the museum, he was young
and stupid then (he always sees himself this way),
but his beloved rouses him, this is why
he buys the milkshake, it's for her.

At a rodent-proof trashcan near a couple
fondling on a bench, he removes the lid and she licks it.
He rips open the cup, she laps up the last of the milkshake,
he slides it down the trashcan's chute.
Past the couple she tugs him to an open gate
where he frees her to high-tail some lost scent inside the park wall.
A scent, some lost scent,

    so long ago,   when I   when

The Retreat

This sound in his head is like an elegant typeface arranging itself
on the base of the line. He doesn't know what that means
but this is the closest he's gotten. Or maybe the sound
is more than just sound, maybe it's spatial, social,
the way we're supposed to organize ourselves. Yes,
the blends of that sound, bitter, sweet, the shifting
alignments peeled away, folded atop one another, like a bite
through the skin to get to the flesh of an orange.

Such are his thoughts as he gets out of bed to pee one night
and, because he doesn't want to disturb his brain
or rather what is in it while he slept, he doesn't turn on the light,
wants those dreamy reflections to lie inside him
undisturbed, moldering, vinegaring, damn, he can't think
of a word to describe it, and just as the word
is about to leap from his mouth, the dark room is flooded
in fluorescence, not a shadow anywhere, his nakedness
there to see. But this light is more than visual, it's a burning
he can touch, another blasted feeling, here we go with feelings,
though the sear of shame is all he can put to words.

He pictures his mother seeing him here, a ribbon of toilet tissue
dangling from his hand between spread legs as she whispers,
"Like a woman." He knows he should defend himself
but "This is just about the base of that line" makes no sense
when what's going on now is these few dribbles, this sidelight
to his thinking, and all she could see is the limp tissue
that he'll wrap around his dick to wear while he's asleep.
"While you sleep?" he can hear her spit at him, no gentleness now
though in his mind her gentleness lingers, but why does he think
of his mind and not his brain, why this sharp turn
from physical to emotional? Or is this actually spiritual?

Maybe he should describe the music of Horace Silver or Monteverdi,
but now he suspects that the sound may be more an abstraction,
a fill-in for what he's been trying to put into words
someone can understand, only he's alone here,

there's no one with him, no mother, as he tosses the tissue
into the bowl, pulls his sweatpants up. "Oh, leave the dribbles
to your sleep," he thinks or says or…what?—there's
not a sound from him, no sound at all, the bowl unflushed.

The light has settled now onto a man, dear old Boyce, who too
has leakage, he could feel fresh droplets of him underfoot,
his own bare foot, when he approached the bowl to sit.
They're here in this lodging far from the habitual balance
of their lives, stirred by everything, which is why he can
actually say now, not in his head but pushed out from his lips
into the space around him, oh all that treasured space,
as he bends over his electronic tablet two-fingering
every word of this into a file he'll send off into that weird space
we've created, send to himself to reclaim tomorrow
when he finishes this, that is the sleep, and he has seen
through the sleep to the sound at last, to this man
named Boyce catching him on the toilet at 4 am.

But it's a sound, remember, not the meaning but the sound
of the word, which his departed friend Robert called the L-word
as if it were an expletive, though he also said,
"I'll try it on for size," and it fit right, he said it did,
then never spoke the word again,
so maybe the sound is not the word but an image
of the way the word sits, that must be it, on a fine-edged
harmonic line, meandering out there
where we actually live, full of mess and distress
at the humiliations of our bodies until, one day, they're gone.

PART THREE

PART THREE

Blue Venom Balls

I.

3 am, a seam of rain and snow, dark
lights, dark asphalt, a streetlamp burning,
leaves down. In day's afterlight
they had glowed, warm
as much as colorful,
now a cold grey underfoot.

A man, a dog cross the street
hike uphill along the park.
The dog's name is the man's father's
nickname, a stand-in
for his given name, Joy, passed on to his son
Robert Joy, killed in Vietnam, 1967.
The man, old now, counts his years by what
remains, though he'll ever
be five years that brother's junior.

Their Joy was hidden on the nameplate
on the front door, J.A., the school principal,
the family in the living room
watching tv, a car stopping out front, voice
screaming "Jackass" for J.A.,
tires digging up a clatter of gravel,
all eyes on the tv still.
Nothing said. It was 1954,
so much unsaid, so little yet to say.

II.

We move along through mounds
of shadow off parked cars, the darkness fizzling
as each streetlamp hoves into view.
I stop to look behind but no one
never anyone, just us

and a street-cleaning sign spray-painted
with vertical letters on the standard
beneath: bluevenomballs

I stare at the words: balls, blue balls
venom balls, the hairy balls of the Haberlock kid
caught on barbed wire running naked
from the lake, farm boys, their big hands
measured for class rings, was it
Hartley who said "Such itty bitty lady fingers,"
or did I tell myself that in my memory,
the way the outside seeps inside
becoming part of me, the backseat guy, sometimes out
sometimes in, effete nonathlete
aka "student manager," those boys wanted me
to bag their wet towels and stinky jockstraps
but I get to sit at the scorer's table, call in the results
to the *Fargo Forum* though of course Dad
doesn't approve and of course I do it, prideful on the phone
so how did I wind up in a car
across from Loring Park, Minneapolis, 1965, a dueling
pistol in my gut, and does that man
really say "Freeze!" and later the cop say
"Do you go to Loring Park often?" ha! where I'll meet
that dark, elegant soldier on leave and horny,
he made a bed for us on newspapers in the park,
was that first love? when I call him later
but his sister answers and I babble nervously
he calls back and says, "What did you say to her?
She said you sounded feminine,"
as I sink into the black receiver in my hand
the outside inside, deeper.

III.

Three houses on the left, a few lights on
always on, some days garbage outside but never a soul
going in or coming out, sad stilted houses

stuck out from the hill, below them more houses
some with wraparound porches, garrets,
you like porches and garrets
but lonely down there, feral cats,
a loop of road lightly trafficked to the train station,
maybe a few blue balls heading home to the grande dames
of Fieldston where the Kennedys once lived

but you're home now and Jocki (after Jock, for Joy)
sits on the floor eyeing the spoon of tiramisu
as it slides into your mouth, you've
been waiting for this all day, such lightness
the way the ladyfingers decompose into soft layers
between the mascarpone, that cold wet walk
history now as you lean down and scratch
her chin, hard to do this, acid in your gut, joints
unyielding while she licks a hint of cream
from your finger, how
you love her but how incomplete
this seems now, like life,
incomplete and,
almost, done.

The Happy Hour

Minneapolis, 1964, downtown alley, dark dead end,
Goldwater time. (Ticking clock, girl with daisy plucking
petals, "3-2-1" in the President's drawl—Fission!)
So much to fear, too young to know how to dodge it.

He's fled The Happy Hour, which adjoins The Gay 90s,
shared back door—you can enter one to go into the other.
The Gay 90s, drag shows, cabaret, the other, men
only, Canoe cologne, ascots, 7&7 on the rocks.

His glands don't work right, no sense of style, no smile,
no third eye, and he hates 7-Up, hates Seagram's 7
(what his dad always stashed in the closet), hates
men, really, the source of his flock-minded misery.

The drag queens with their shellacked eyelids and lips
scare him more than walking through The Happy Hour's
front door or leaving that way into the warm summer
night's brief interval between winters, no time to waste.

His feet scrape alley cement, in the gloom, two men
together, one plain, the other muscled, they seem safe,
the muscled one nods him over (anything for muscles),
pushes him to his knees, says "Not just me—him too,"

hands on his shoulders, the two men kiss ('This is love?'
he thinks) as they pass him from one to the other, rough,
rougher, he's in a pliant fog (minutes? hours?), then he's
back in The Happy Hour, the lights burst on. Last call.

For All Time

I hear a voice a man's voice a boy's well maybe not
who can tell it's coming in like shortwave through bad weather
out here in the North Atlantic the thinnest
strip of land holding me in tow
to the continent we lived on this voice
and I landlocked dead center and I know the voice a boy's
a man's a friend's a soldier's a
dare I say it lover's voice
as I waken now and it crashes on me like the car he rolled
off the gravel on Route 1 the father's car the teacher's car the enforcer's
where I see this boy this man in its front seat blood on his forehead
though he survived we all survived depending on how
you measure it but then who stays intact
not the lover not that love
the tease of it a morsel suspended
before my eyes my lips he standing naked in the steam
behind the bathroom door showing me the enormous red
boil high on his thigh below what I can't
take my eyes from or stretched out on his bed combing the hair
on the legs of the man he's so proud to be he lets me see
but I never dare to touch or in truth never succeed
in touching until he touches me, he did touch me in that dream
I know is real the touch at last the sliding down and around
of his mouth so shocking and sweet but before its
pleasure can be real that burst that rupture that wordless
wall my wall hard for me to talk
those silent years of shock and yet a thawing is that
love the moving on from a sore limb
to a good one we two eyeing our
faces our shared faces eyes father mother bed
me curled on my couch he and his wife in my bedroom brand-new
pillows too when she tells me I sleep like a little boy
and he smiles those days before he's shipped away way out
way over though he will come back he
does come back finally back a profile on white
satin framed in wood.

Before Stonewall After

It was a plain dark down stairway leading off West 10th,
a truck driver's-side mirror pointed up the stairs,
the code words *shotzie* or *midget*
bartender whispered to a voice behind the door
in hopes that it would open.

When it does, *voila!,* the Snake Pit—on the old cement
a circular bar is centered in the room, its floor sunken inside it
so, yes, the bartenders are midgets, maybe we all are,
Nixon's president, this is how we do social.

Morey brought me here, heard about it
on the rounds of bars we frequented down
to the foot of Christopher, the elevated West Side Drive
hulking there, good place for those with nowhere
else to bring the evening's pleasure.

A sudden bang and crack, young man standing
at the door, finger to his lips, axe blade slicing wood,
sharp-ended crowbars, the door bursts
open, cops flood through.

No back door, the midgets say *Sit tight*, emptying
the cash drawers, we all take the hint, clear
pockets of drugs and pot and poppers, Morey yells
My career! My career! though he hates every job he's ever had,
me, I'm just a temp, hoping I can get back into NYU.

We're herded up the stairs, queued at the gutter,
the cops poke a few chests with nightsticks but seem
to have lost interest in this group of queers,
let us go as if it's a favor, I stumble home.

~~~

A night out drinking Beautifuls (scotch and Benedictine),
down, he'd been down so long now, haunting
the same old Village joints, wanting what, another
night not to end as miserably as the last?

His lover punched him in the face, a guy he'd brought home
pulled a gun on him, he calls his shrink at midnight,
calls friends in California too, earlier there, he doesn't want
those he knows right here to see him keep
doing what he doesn't want them to see him do.

He leaves the Trilogy twinks for the leather joints
down on the Hudson, never has any luck there
but down he goes to West Street, the Ramrod, another
place to drink and watch a game of pool.

Reagan just got elected, but it's the usual crowd
until a burst of bullets blasts through the window,
everyone hits the floor, the pool players too,
and as he rises and heads out the door
one of them still lies there, dying.

On the sidewalk footprints in red head
to Christopher, he follows them, stumbling
around the corner until they fade
and he's back at Trilogy, blackout as usual.

"You're drinking a lot," a friend tells him, his tongue
curled on the L as if to underscore it, so
he stops calling him, stops calling everyone,
months pass, he sees a headline in the *New York Times*:
Rare Cancer Seen in 41 Homosexuals.

Wilderness

The fog is dense, even a short Manhattan street block gets lost
until he reaches its end, his is a long avenue block, totally
veiled as he steps onto it, praying that the brown bag will still be there
on the sidewalk where he left it twenty minutes ago.
Who'd be out in this, he thought, a betrayal of his motive, the point
being to get rid of what he couldn't bring himself to pour down
the drain: These last twenty minutes were all he could wait.

And it's open, anyone can see, who'd take an open jug
of anything left on a New York street? For one thing, it's cheap,
no way he'd indulge in French Bordeaux, this is just
Classic California Red, no, no one would stoop to take it, besides
if God doesn't want me to have it, then it won't still be there, although
that's bullshit, he thinks, until he sees it sitting on the street.

A woman emerges from the fog. Don't stop, please don't stop,
he thinks, and for a second it looks as if she won't, but she lifts
the bag and draws the bottle all the way out where she can see it,
slides it right back in as if to set it on the ground, then quickly
tucks it under her arm, bag and all, passing by in the streetlight.

She disappears into the fog, he slams his way inside the door,
marches up the stairs, cursing, one flight, two, slows to a stop,
sits on a stair in the hallway light, taking in what just took place.

An Iceless Arctic

I'm reading the headline aloud over our burgers at McDonald's
when she says, "But what if you don't believe it's melting?—
I don't," oh, I know she admires Bush *fils* but I take care

to avoid politics, we talk about ballet, opera, she takes
a cinema class each Thursday, supports marriage equality
for chrissake, now she sounds as if she just blew in from Boise,

how can I be friends with a know-nothing in denial, though
I've always liked her, sitting alone on a log with her dog
in what we call The Woods, a nod, a smile, and a few weeks

and real words later we're friends, both older than we want
to admit, though we talk about everything, things I don't tell
just anyone—"I never drank Pinot Grigio," I once announced,

"I chewed it"—she laughs at my jokes, draws more out of me
than I intend to share, while she's filled me in on all the sex
she had in Europe, brings her Brittany every day, but none of that

love talk with him like what I do with my Welsh terrier, she likes
that he's aloof, looking off into the trees nobly, I've brought scones,
corn muffins, fed him my decaf, he even licked my nose once,

and she's got a crush on a man—"crush," that's what she said—
paints her toenails, brushes on a touch of blush, oh Maddy
how can I expel another friend from my rigid, righteous circle?

Provincetown Song

The water begins here, a mottle of blue
amid green reeds, hills of sand
covered with beech trees, the two-lane road
beneath me draped with power lines,
a large transformer at eye level
and beyond, a flat of blue bay water where
I see a rim of mainland through the haze.

A microclimate here, moisture air-borne
on a chill sea breeze this early hour, rust
rampant on that transformer stepping down
the flow of current that keeps this computer on,
lights the rooms at night, powers the AC
I run only when the midday sun
blasts right through these windows.

I watch the Boston ferry hustle by,
it looks risky from my point of view,
too close to land or speeding high above
amid fragile bits of white sail out there,
bikers, walkers, the town's street vacuum,
a Porsche, its top down, have drifted by,
oblivious to the water that surrounds us.

An odd marriage of images in this town
where marriage burst upon us, women wed
women, men men, genders benders, straights
(them too) straights, and families, dogs, the love
that dare not speak its name all gather here
at this tip of sand where drifters linger, seeking
whatever's to be found at this land's end.

I'm old, but today I feel young, foolish, guilty,
sopping up this electric juice from the grid
that grasps us in its greed yet makes so much
possible across that flatland of water,
an angst that turns my own end to
a reverie as I ease free of this land, our
land, which all that blue soon may claim.

Hands

I call him Papi. He leans hunch-backed
across the table, viewing the balls lying there grave
and motionless after the break. Peels his hands
from the table's edge, large hairy hands, unpacks
his cue, winks at me standing by his jacket on the floor,
then spits in his hands, holding them aloft like an offering,

or a command.
                       She lies on the couch naked, offering
her little body, me in my underwear, backed
into this corner I've created. Angela—I eye the floor
of her belly, the frightening slit, grave,
blue-veined. Bald too, and when I rub the clothed pack
of my crotch against it she puts her hands

on my hips, tugs my shorts down, hands
myself to me above her, it's bare and shrunk, offering
nothing. I don't know how to pack
up my ignorance, I don't know why I want to back
away from the lip of some kind of grave
a voice is telling me not to near.
                                 He floors

the gas pedal, turns the corner, dumps me to the floor
and pulls the handbrake on. Hands
me a joint, I take a drag, grave
and brave in my daring. A stranger's offerings
are not common, and I won't back
down, not now, as he unpacks

the hard-on from his trousers. Unpacks
me too, spreads me across the truck's floor
face up, legs up, his arched back
pumping at the air, hands
clamped to my shoulders, not one offering
of affection, just this need, this grave

hunt for pleasure.
             Now here I am, wailing at a grave,
a man's I barely knew. Father Carl unpacks
his holy water and sprinkles everything, offering
I don't know what kind of peace. At the floor
of the grave I see my father's hands
opening in the darkness of the coffin.
                              Back

in the church basement we eat baked
ham and cheese sandwiches. How grieved
the day's become—a few rain clouds, the bands
of the clock tightening. "Uncrack
your books to hymn 43," Father had said. At the door
the coffin sat, another wicked one's suffering.

PART FOUR

Grit

> *The history of my stupidity would fill many volumes.*
> — Czeslaw Milosz, "Account," tr. Robert Pinsky

I spend my days choosing between a and the,
parsing thin layers in the history
of meaning, this yellowed map that precedes me. Of
it, it seems I know so little, and my
pride, purple nugget of stupidity,
tugs me into wars with *should* and *would*
as hot, fat, black urges un-fill
my heart. Oh, how remorse hunts down so many
of my best humors! Then, a silence. The silence. Volumes.

Grown Men

I was 48 when it got Ray,
a grown man, he went early,
& Dennis & Duncan & Arlie, all
early, so many gone so soon,

but that was then, now
22 years later, you
may be going early
too. We've made a big
mistake. It isn't over
(what part of 'it' is it?)

& grown men don't grow,
they're born that way,
aren't they? So what is this dis-
ease? Jeez, don't go too.

draped on the bed

it had fallen
open when he
fell asleep
the robe's white
brilliance across
grey elastic
stockings tight
around bloated
thighs when i
walk into his room
and beneath bald
pubes see
with a jolt
of curious
desire
the effect
of his edema
meaty, vital
this irony
of nature
the rest left lie

Moules Frites
for R.H.

The mound of steaming shells glistens black, the pink and beige
fruit inside each one unable to evade my eye, or my fork
as I reach in, loosen the flesh, which clings just enough to know
they are indeed, as the waiter claimed, "fresh as you can get,"

though it's curious I have this craving, I'd never liked mussels
or rather hadn't given them much thought until I saw you quiz
the waiters with such care before you ordered and when they
were then set down on our table, how lustily you ate them up.

As in Provincetown, June, the film festival, I can see you now
in that French tub, an island in our bathroom, sunk in water
above your shoulders, inhaling the scent of the herbal salts,
you wrote a poem about it, and when we paused in our hop

from film to film, you handed me a copy, which I loaded on
my computer, pasting it over a photo of that bathtub, empty,
the salty water drained away, and right across its foot the last
lines of your poem: *Soapless saltless endless end of me...*

One day back home many years later, I filled my own tub,
dumped in the salts you'd given me, what a release to lie there,
their grit dissolving beneath my butt, the distant June days,
all those fresh plump mussels we pried from their dark shells

like these I'm having now, their flesh awash in garlic broth, me
dipping the coarse bread in too, just as you'd do. How I cling
to these fleet remnants of your presence when, despite the pain
your absence awakes, still I rejoice that you're never quite gone.

Doesn't

His dog knew he was leaving when he packed the jar,
silly jar but handsome, big black round lid resting
on four clear square shoulders. Once it held jam but
now it's capsules, psyllium, baby aspirin, whatever
he knows he needs to take each day, but doesn't.

What is this about *doesn't*? People lack compassion,
their eyes drain when he speaks of it, the things he
doesn't do anymore. Doesn't want to do, can't/won't
do. Like sex. Dishes. Phone calls. The next breath.

Ah, a good stiff drink, a chair reclined, one more
slice of pizza have much to praise as mental fatigue
sinks to the soles of his feet, aches where he touches
ground, where he's stood all these years, alone.

Well, some of them alone. But even when he's not,
that intransigence of solitude. His own personal
doughnut hole everything revolves around. *Who,
what can replenish me?* Bad habit. Dies hard.

He left his dog behind and he and the jar flew away,
it seemed so easy—drop her off, take off. Then
her photo arrived by text. She didn't look so good.
Head down. Tail too. It preys on his mind, still.

His bed is empty, though onto it he clings; his
jar sits on its own shelf, empty too. Next to him
his dog watches as he swallows his day's meds.
He looks down, she yawns. It comes to him that
it takes breath to yawn. He smiles, yawns too.

Pathways

Her left hand is in a small box, open-ended, a mirror on its right side facing her right hand, a bit of a claw after years of arthritis but now the good hand—and it moves, which the mirror reflects as she tries to get her left hand to mimic the right in hopes of stimulating neural pathways to replace the ones the stroke erased.

It's like piggybacking, he tells her, wondering if she ever carried him piggyback, he's sure his dad never did, nor most likely his mom, but did she, his sister, nine years his senior, obliged to look after him, as in the trips they took to Swedlund's up North Hill outside town, where he told her he'd marry her when he grew up.

Growing up was grisly, he thinks, unlearning the cringe-worthy and taking on new airs, like when he was old enough for college and fancied himself free, she paid the tuition his father said he couldn't afford, he crossed a threshold then, he her dependent, their childhood bond now tinged adult, in some way grey.

But she was a friend, a mentor, introduced him to Drambuie, Vivaldi, *Le nozze di Figaro*, Chateaubriand, Cutty Sark, so much he'd known nothing about as he wriggled off his small-town life to take on a new one out East where, well, he ended up a drunk but sobered up, ten years later helping her get to detox.

After their mother died, she called him, wanted to jump off Lake Street Bridge, she said, could he come help, and he arrived to a mountain of unopened mail on her dining table, in her freezer the magnum of vodka whose level he marked each day, then left her in the detox, angry, hostile, yet they stay close, so close.

Ah, neural pathways, he thinks, mine have frayed too, may they hold up enough to help carry her through, and they laugh as she strains to turn the sweatshirt she put on backwards right-side round while he times how long it takes, "Just seven minutes thirty-one seconds, all by yourself," he says, "Bravo, brava!" She beams.

Marilyn in Minnesota

The young stag's hooves shine in the daylight,
his rack has some way yet to grow, and his ears
are slender, erect, their movement so slight
in the wind, which at his speed must be fierce,
me going sixty on I-494
as the SUV passes me, him tied
to the deck on its rear end while I speed
to catch up, only when I get there
it's time to pull off on France Avenue
up to Fairview's intensive care, you
on the top floor like last year, this next
event of what I know has been too many,
oh how I wish we could help you be
granted, too, that last moment of rest.

So Tender an Hour

It's 2 am, and I thought outside
was where we would meet,
but he's in the vestibule (exterior
door not bolted) so I'm obliged to step
through the inside door to the claustrophobic
light in which he's standing, tall
and lithe, dark red hair
thick as velvet, his open
hand extended my way, a warm
clasp I cling to not too long I hope
as through the door the man then
wends the gurney to the lift.

Upstairs, her dog is still on the bed, bony
and atremble, nested loyal
at her side, all week at her side, save
to seek out food and a little water.
Yes, a little water, Q-tips of it spread
across her lips. "This is the way," she had said—
in her home, no more attempts to repair
the irreparable—though not everyone agrees.

But sweet her caregivers were to wait
for me to fly back at midnight,
declining to strand dog and body and
leave me to arrive alone,
though I'm fine now while this man and I talk,
curious at how one goes about this
at so tender an hour. He raises
the gurney even with the bed to spread
that bag wide open and slides her
onto it with his big red hands
chatting I don't know what with
the same grace and surety in which he moves,
my dear sister's body shuttered now
in that bag with one hushed zip.

Text to Text

why that blah blah blah in your text
i just woke to from two hours' sleep
on the couch after my day-long
trip to boston to meet mary,
she a chance to see my jocki,
first time since puppyhood, an odd
lunch we had at legal sea food
craving rainbow trout but there was
none, just a tired waitress whose
nose ring looked like what I soon found
in my roasted mushrooms (crab cake
free for me!), mary paid the check,
i tipped twenty bucks, and how we
laughed and talked, about you of course,
the first mary heard of your quick
move to boise, and though the dear
old girl didn't say so, her gifts
of food to jocki (so tender)
spoke loudly this might be the last
parting, she wouldn't hug goodbye,
she by uber, jocki and i
by ferry back to provincetown,
a sloppy bounce through wind and waves,
worse as we got close to town, when
suddenly the boat pitched awry
(spray on all the windows), cups, plates
sliding off tables, young couple
some rows up springing up, fussing
with their baby, the carriage, clothes,
mother furiously wiping,
father grimacing through his nose
when at last we passed the light at
the tip of long point, gentling in
to macmillan pier's stiff arm, a
line of the soon-to-be-surprised
awaiting the crossing back, near
darkness now, a quick drive for some

late pizza at spiritus, film
festival folk hogging the front
of the garden as we hunkered
in the corner, then at home, faint,
i passed out on the couch, jocki

faithful next to me, coming to
to your text, woozy, is this from
the crossing or some kind of stroke
or an allergy to shellfish,
what, i wonder, and why fight it,
my dog's enough, isn't she, we
all will die or at least drift off,
you, to idaho, blah blah blah

Love

Her head droops in the Elizabethan collar,
a clear plastic cone that keeps her from chewing
her stitches, she might have died, often he dreams
she's dead, or dying, or stolen, trapped in a fire,
thrown off a cliff, sometimes he even thinks
he himself could do it. Can that be? Real fathers, real
mothers surely don't consider killing their own.

His was always working, struggling with her health,
the three meals a family expects each day but
an artist too, in paint or yarn, even whipped wax,
then she'd turn, debowel a chicken, stick her hand
down a toilet drain, a woman of hands, not head,
like his father. After he died, one day she announced,
"Who'd ever have believed we'd last so long?"

His father was cold, removed, nested with his pipes,
his cheap tobacco, crammed and blind in a daily
grind of duty, habit, his Seagram's in the kitchen
cupboard, on a shelf in his closet, its stink often even
in the bathroom water glass, all the smoky silent
hours his son himself will no longer do, forked
off from his father now, abandoned to his own urges.

He removes the cone, she sags even further, how
he'd looked forward to her return, hearing her
yelp and growl prodding him to play but old now,
frail, needs help mounting his bed, will go way
before he goes. In his head an image arises: she,
flung off Henry Hudson Bridge, her ears lifted into
tiny sails, paws down, bellying the dark water.

PART FIVE

Fine Arts Work Center

Often I bump my head, sharp corners,
the slant of walls becoming ceilings,
and so it was this morning I arose
from the commode pivoting east as I did,
my head just grazing the skylight's recess,
eyes trained on a nuclear sight freighted
in reds and oranges, a chemical stew

of sun not quite arisen as we hurried
out the door, it was 5 a.m., barely
slippers on my feet, she being dog
happy to join me away out here
on Commercial Street devoid of any
traffic, people, no one but us, she
off leash, tail up searching, searching,
could she be sensing my odd unease—

up here at sea in this artifice of life,
she dozing on the morning chair, blanket
hilled to her liking, so composed yet
alert to the slightest change in our tone
of conversation, the object of this time
spent here, we talk about ways to talk
for the best effect of the silent worlds
we display on pages such as these—

but soon the color drains, the sun rises,
cool humid air absorbing my nuked
illusion, though the sun's nuclear fusion
is the source of life, little furry one
at my feet street-sweeping scents to
prompt her morning's relief, I can read
each hint, I've come to adore this way
we communicate, this silent speak.

Another Summer

It's my twentieth one here, Sophie and
her sister Monique glow as I order
a cheese slice, a Greek one too, my usual,
while without my asking, Frankie has my
iced tea ready, and Wencz the wizardly
pizza-crust man at rest in the back booth
waves a knobby hand, he had surgery
on his lip, he says, but two months later
it's still numb, his wife made him do it, I
frown a kind of smile, set down my slices
on a backyard table, pull off a hunk
of crust for my dog, "basal surgery,"
he'd said, but what's this empty bottle here?
Cabernet sauvignon. The label reads
"Requiem." Thirty summers I've been free.

Into the Valley

This is California, isn't the buzzword here PC,
                                   so who insists on calling it that word?
Over half a century since my last trip here,
                                   16 then, and though in the 1960
Olympics no one objected to the valley's name,
                                   still I knew that word wasn't kindly.

Take 'squaw point,' outside my hometown in North Dakota,
                             where we drove to get our booze, the catchall name
for the sod and wood cabin two old drunks
                                       lived in with their 'native' women.
There was, too, Mrs. Davis, who strode off the prairie
                             into town to get supplies, schoolkids taunting her.

She seemed beyond human, surreal, I imagined her
                             dematerialized outside town, awaiting
each next visit, her dark skin, masculine gait,
                                       a fierce determination.
Pride, perhaps, and some of the Norwegian locals,
                           watching her arrive, would let out a muted *Uf-ta*.

Here, the valley is now settled. Houses are scattered
                                   across the mountain meadows,
one-lane asphalt splits off the state highway
                           down into broken forests, up toward bare cliffs,
the Sierra Nevada closing in on both sides,
                           rising to that namesake peak at valley's end.

Forgive the name! I tell myself. It's just a word.
                               But on this day I arrive, summer 2016,
I'm afraid we're stuck in a pit of bitter words
                                   that defy all convention, and I find myself
sapped of restraint, of civility which I fear,
                           once it's completely gone, will not readily return.

The 'Village' has a German look, a folksy street
                            that could be from a set for *Die Meistersinger*,
though the parking lot beyond is pure Americana,
                            and those mountains above, dry, awaiting
years of missing snow, wondering, if mountains do,
                        whatever's become of what we thought we knew?

Gathered

Highway 15 wasn't paved back then, a
dusty country road with graveled shoulders,
easy to flip a car into the ditch
if you weren't careful, which I wasn't, so
down into it I and my mother landed.

She was teaching me to drive, unlike my
siblings I was lucky my father didn't bother
with me, she a gentle soul beneath her farmgirl
surface. We were able to back out, shaken,
when she said, "Let's drive down to Peterson's."

It was a dam, not much, in a gully
the Sheyenne River lazed through, a little
slit in the flat, farmed prairie, enough
trees grown full for shade, a pool with fish
and though no one ever came here,

this day it was a pleasure, my mother
sitting on the ground above the dam, me
eager to get back on the road driving
but, the dust of our arrival settled,
I settled with her too by the falling water,

well, flowing anyway, a few birds, the
splash of what may have been a fish gulping
down a dragonfly, there were many, some
daytime crickets, hardly the wild my mother
loved, we still had some wild left then before

it was all declared gone, but this respite we'd
found so near home, it was man-made, as if
penance for breaking the sod up there,
unleashing the soil, often blown away, here
we two sat, silent in the sounds, gathered.

My Mother's Breasts

Auntie Edna—or Annie, which we'd come
to call her—was driving us nuts, her husband
had died and my mother was obliged to spend
the spring with her over-tidy, bossy
oldest sister, who my mother claimed
she let name all us children, as if
to make up for Annie having none,

and by the time my father and I arrived,
Annie was cleaning ashtrays beneath burning
cigarettes, cooking up new chores (hedges,
breezeway, basement) for us to do (my father
was exempted), but on this day Annie,
my mother and I, lunch over, were still
sitting at the table, Annie sucking air
through a gap between her teeth, as she'd do

after every meal. "You can't make that sound,
Allie, can you?" Allie. Alice. My mother.
She rose and said, "Well, here's a sound Annie
can't make." She grasped her blouse between thumb
and forefinger chest-high, tugged the fabric
out before her, jumped straight up, and with
each jump a smack of flesh against flesh, not
slap or clap, more like the sound of raw dough

in her hands, a sound I, thirteen then, had
heard my entire life as she'd pat out dough
for loaves of bread, trays of cinnamon rolls,
soft, muffled, watering my mouth as I
watched her bake, sometimes moody, sometimes
gay, not that look on her face now, little
sister's get-even I supposed, only
this time I saw just Edna and Alice, no
auntie, no mother anywhere in sight.

On We Went

Just we two took the trail to the Tea House,
a long climb through dense forest, breaks
in the trees revealing how high we'd gone,
Lake Louise a distant sapphire blue.

On we went, my mother and I, just up and went,
no father, he didn't share my mother's passion
for the wild, nor did I except when I was
actually with her, at a picnic table, say, her
leg bent, hands clasped around her knee.

We weren't going the entire route but on we went,
it had been a rainy day, so good to be out,
or perhaps it was inertia, drawn by a call
simply to see what was around the next bend.

We reached the Tea House, perched on bare rock
above us, had I suggested going in for a bite to eat
or some tea, I wonder if my mother, not
the tea-drinking type, might have gone on in.

But I didn't, so on we went, down the trail now,
a fast descent, just the two of us when around a bend
we saw them, *Bears!* my mother whispered,
and there they were on the trail, one atop the other.

We made noises, quiet ones, loud ones, no results.
"Should I throw a rock?" I said, and when I did, off
the trail they ran. "I think they were more interested
in each other" was all my mother said, on we went.

Forty years later, the two of us on a slab of rock,
Cambria, California, you grasping a beachcombing
cane as always, I finally tell you what I feel bad I've
never said: "Mom, I'm gay." You look surprised and
I hurry on to say, "Don't worry, I don't have AIDS."

That was it, on we went until that night, you came
into my room, sat on my bed, took a bit of blanket
in your hand and said, "I love you." That was it.
Did I say I love you, too?

Brother Eyes

I don't like touching him, the MRSA daunts me,
haunts every corner of this room, his house, my
clothes, my dog's fur, we standing here at the foot
of his bed watching the peace in which he seems

to lie, then all at once his eyes pop open,
I want to leave but fear he sees me, his eyes
escaping from the 'sleep' he lives in now,
though this is daylight, 'life' as we know it.

I try to smile, his eyes grow large, larger
than I remember, hazel I'd call them, they
have no pure color, green taking in the room,
blue resting on me now—on me!—as

he smiles, bright, brighter, and the angst I feel
never having truly known him, at last now perhaps

for this one and only time. . .
evaporates.

for good

i was trying to take money from sis's estate, you said,
to make a film no less (how could you know that
fifty years ago i wanted to make films?) in paris i
nearly outstayed my visa to do *un projet avec jérôme*,
i guess i was in love with him, but where were you,
ten years older and a freight-train bum whom
the cops pulled off some high-wire lines in LA
and stuck in the loony bin where they put you
on thorazine, one brief stop on your life-long tour
of druggy drunken ways to fuck up your life leaving
anyone who got close to you bating breath until
the next disappearance, or appearance, both
pretty much the same, so what could you know
of me from those pop-in visits when you would
take up some cool thing like ant-collecting, i cut
my legs on barbed wire traipsing with you over
the prairie hunting ants down then tossed them
out when you took off again, always an *again* but
never a *for good* until dad died, you skipped the
funeral of course, but the *for good* finally arrived,
you lived with mom for twenty years, that's right,
and how much sis and i appreciated it, though in
mom's decline when i told her how she hurt you
when she told you she was afraid you'd leave for
greener grass, she thought a moment, said "he'll
never find anything greener than he's got right here,"
for god's sake why do we keep hurting one another,
and yes between excursions for the ants i shouldn't
have told you to go out and get a job and yes i knew
the disease and the meds are what got you paranoid
and forgive me if letting your caregiver sneak you
into that jewish cemetery was against your wishes
(who could ever really know your wishes?) it's
over, done with, we should all forgive one another,
me especially, me alone here now, all by myself

Paco, Brother, and Me

Little brother looks at the photo of his brother's Lab
wearing tinted swimming goggles in his brother's pool,
only it's not his brother's pool and not
his brother's dog anymore, not even his brother.
That man in the pool with Paco
is the husband of Consuelo, she was his brother's
keeper. How quickly things change hands!

The Parkinson's, the MRSA in the rift in his leg
where they'd cut him open to pin the femur straight—
little brother regards the photo more closely,
the husband's pale legs beneath the water, his
short thick dark hands gentled around Paco's neck,
chest chastely clothed in a blue t-shirt, cheek
pressed to Paco's ear, face tanned, a strip
of lighter skin where a hat band must have rested.

Juan did odd jobs around the house, a man of faith too,
Consuelo said he led her church, some kind
of Christian-Jewish faith, she waved her hand as if
the story was too long, too hard to explain.
He cooked good Mexican fare quietly in the kitchen
far from little brother's brother as Consuelo and
Crisanta, a member of their church, did their tending.

They always asked little brother to join them for their meals,
clasped hands with him and said short prayers
in Spanish and Hebrew and English but
he was lost, sister had just died,
all this in his hands alone now, a brother he never
fully knew, and a peek into this new, disarming clan.

Little brother had flown in for what he thought
would be the end, only brother didn't die, but it was time
to be practical, what would brother want them to do
with his things (the house he'd left to Consuelo),
what about the furniture, the books and papers,

his mother's paintings Consuelo had found stashed
in the garage and persuaded brother
to let her hang, and when the time came,
his remains, she'd talked to brother about it, he'd said
she could do whatever she wanted, and she wanted
a burial in a Jewish cemetery nearby, where she could
watch over him after he died.

Little brother was stunned, but he listened,
and so they go to the cemetery and are shown
where brother could be buried, Consuelo will share the plot,
then off to the mortuary, how to handle this
non-Jew's ceremony, Consuelo fills out the story of her family,
great, great-great, great-great-great grandparents
back in Acapulco, their names, their histories,
a story about someone plucking a chicken and twirling it
over her head by its feet then cooking and giving it to the poor,
little brother's sure they'll be thrown out but rabbi's eyes
light up, he says Consuelo's family must have come
from the Spanish expulsion, some came to the Caribbean,
Mexico, even Brazil, "Have you ever been to Brazil?" he asks,
"They have great food!" then calls the cemetery, a brief chat,
hangs up the phone and says, "It's kosher!"

I look at the photograph again, sweet and clumsy Paco
in those silly goggles, the water soft and calm,
Juan inscrutable in his wet t-shirt
which across its chest I now can see reads EVERLAST.

The Keepers

You had been our keeper—John, Marilyn, me.
Dad and Bob too, so long gone. Oh, yes,
J did live with you, but you know he was
disabled many ways, and M and I, we
lived thousands of miles away. "Can't I stay
at home?" you cried, "I'll be good." What to say?

The search: wheelchairs in hallways, disheartening
till we found Shirley. A nurse, like your daughter,
but retired. You her patient then, in her sole care.
Did you mind she called you Mom, tempering
you, I still fancy, leaving you to pace your end?
It came late for you, too soon for me. I went,

not two months before you died, off to Blenheim,
Glyndebourne, London. Not to you. I'm left with, Why?

Gleason's Beach

So it was I went looking for it, what she, my mother,
loved in Washington and Oregon, not bright
beaches or sun tans but a wildness
of wind, fog, rain, breakers crashing cliffs, fractured
timber washed ashore, empty shells,
stones weathered to a sheen,
a place you had to work at to get there.

A friend in San Francisco told me to try
the Sonoma coast, not far north, a few hours'
drive at most, so here I was at last on Coast Highway
entering Bodega Bay, no real ocean yet,
a harbor, wisps of fog, until I rounded a bend
going uphill out of town, and there it was
through a mix of sun, fog, the coastline chewed
by tides, parts of mainland still standing
beyond the breakers. It was 1980, "This is it," I thought.

Now I'm back, for just the third time since
we spent those summers here, the first
for a reunion with Peter, he'd walked from
New York to California for Feed America Now,
which he'd founded to battle hunger, then
settled on Russian River and died of AIDS soon after,
the second in 1998 to scatter my mother's ashes
on what we'd come to know was called
Gleason's Beach. And now, here on the floor
beside me, my sister's ashes sit.

How good it feels to drive this curving two-lane
road again! The fog crawls up and down
the brown ("Golden, ha!" my mother said) California
hills, a live oak here and there, dense and green, eucalyptus,
and in the clefts of low mountains hidden
stands of redwoods had somehow escaped the axe.

Coast Highway descends a hill, crosses a creek
with no name I know then curves up
the other side past a string of houses put up
50-60 years ago, my mother's rental among them,
but a traffic light out of nowhere pops
into view, the road narrows to one lane, and
as I drive by 'our house' I can see that
the line of houses beyond have fallen into the sea.

I double back to no-name creek, park, walk
my dog and my sister's ashes to Gleason's Beach
right below our house, its seventy-eight steps
long washed away, which stands solid for now
on hard rock that will most likely end up
out beyond the breakers with the ones we admired
all those years ago. But something's changed,

I expected this task would be sad, perhaps
one I shouldn't have taken on, but that
debris of the fallen homes behind me as I scatter
my sister's remains tells me that everything
will change, all the houses' remains
will be down here too, Coast Highway moved
miles inland or even vanished, so
puny we are, facing whatever is in store.

Missive

*Hammer, nail, wood:
the tight echo
through my window,
the way the sound
splits open light,
dispersing seed,
an odd contentment
of yearning.*

*The ripeness of new
lumber, the squeal
of saw, its dustings
underfoot, the moist
dug earth, green beams
uplifting the fragile
community of men,
their swaggering
dance of tools.*

*Yet it's an It,
woodhammernail:
a unitary
missive from
some center,
the weight
of each perfect
verberation
when so little
seems so right.*

ACKNOWLEDGMENTS

I am grateful to the editors of the following publications who have graciously chosen to publish some of the poems in this book:

"Brother Eyes"—*Written Here 2019* (The Community of Writers)
"Dinner, for Two"—*Barrow Street*
"The Drawing"—*Ploughshares*, as "First Encounter"
"Missive"—*Passager*, as "A Kind of Bliss"
"Pathways"—*Written Here 2016* (The Community of Writers)
"Visitors"—*American Arts Quarterly*

Richard **Sime** was born in Bremerton WA and raised in North Dakota. He moved to New York City in 1966 to pursue a Ph.D. in political science but soon dropped out and worked on the Foreign News Desk at the New York Times and on the 1968 presidential campaign of Eugene McCarthy. He settled into educational publishing, where he was an editor for over thirty years, earning an M.F.A. in fiction writing at Sarah Lawrence College in 1994. He left publishing in 2000 and began to write poetry at the Fine Arts Work Center in Provincetown MA. He returns each summer to work with the many poets who gather there, and is also an alumnus of the Community of Writers in Olympic Valley CA. His work has appeared in, among others, *The New Republic, Barrow Street, Ploughshares, Salamander, Provincetown Arts, American Arts Quarterly, Sixfold Poetry,* and *Radical Faerie Digest.* He lives with his Welsh terrier on the bank of the Hudson River in Bronx NY.

www.ingramcontent.com/pod-product-compliance
Lightning Source LLC
Chambersburg PA
CBHW031125160426
43192CB00008B/1120